John McCain

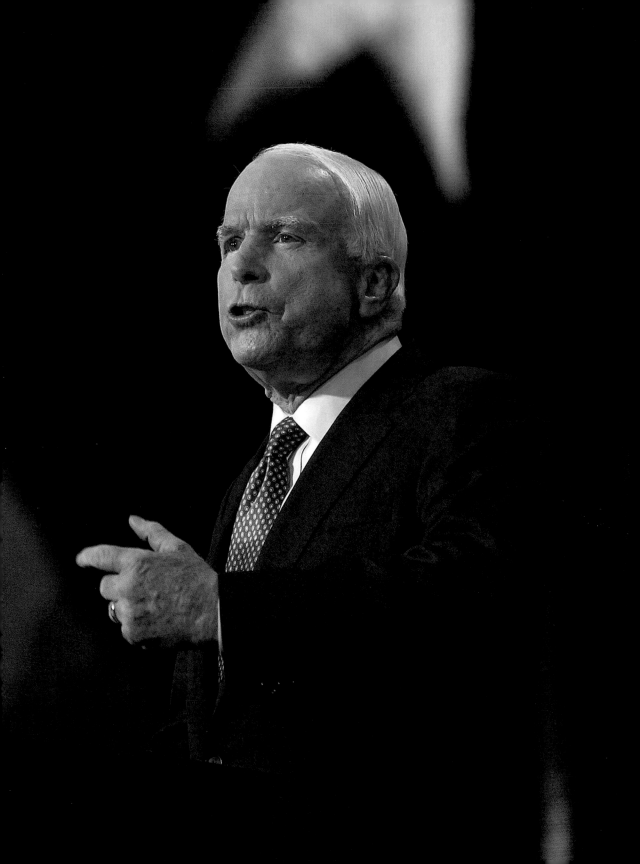

John McCain

THE COURAGE OF CONVICTION

WITHDRAWN

HEATHER E. SCHWARTZ

LERNER PUBLICATIONS ◆ MINNEAPOLIS

Lerner Publications Company
A division of Lerner Publishing Group, Inc.
241 First Avenue North
Minneapolis, MN USA 55401

For reading levels and more information, look up this title at www.lernerbooks.com.
Image credits: John Tlumacki/The Boston Globe/Getty Images, p. 2; Thomas J. O'Halloran/ Library of Congress, pp. 6, 8; Terry Ashe/The LIFE Images Collection/Getty Images, p. 9; Seth Poppel Yearbook Library, pp. 10, 11, 12; Bettmann/Getty Images, p. 14; Corbis Historical/Getty Images, p. 16; AP Photo/Horst Faas, p. 19; CRANDALL/SIPA/Newscom, p. 21; Warren K. Leffler/ Library of Congress (LC-DIG-ppmsca-03128), p. 22; Dick Swanson/The LIFE Images Collection/ Getty Images, p. 23; lauradyoung/E+/Getty Images, p. 25 (Silver Star) (Bronze Star); DNY59/E+/ Getty Images, p. 25 (Purple Heart); PeteHoffmanMN/iStock/Getty Images, p. 25 (Distinguished Flying Cross); Susan Biddle/The Denver Post/Getty Images, p. 27; The Washington Times/ ZUMAPRESS/Newscom, p. 28; AP Photo/Ron Edmonds, p. 29; Karin Cooper/Hulton Archive/ Getty Images, p. 30; HENNY RAY ABRAMS/AFP/Getty Images, p. 31; Carolyn Cole/Los Angeles Times/Getty Images, p. 32; STAN HONDA/AFP/Getty Images, p. 34; Chris Oberholtz/Orlando Sentinel/Tribune News Service/Getty Images, p. 35; Everett Collection/Shutterstock.com, p. 36; Brooks Kraft/Corbis Historical/Getty Images, p. 37; Chip Somodevilla/Getty Images, p. 39; Jonathan Newton/The Washington Post/Getty Images, p. 40.

Cover: Joshua Lott/Getty Images.

Main body text set in Rotis Serif Std 55 Regular 13.5/17. Typeface provided by Adobe Systems.

Library of Congress Cataloging-in-Publication Data

Names: Schwartz, Heather E., author.
Title: John McCain : the courage of conviction / Heather E. Schwartz.
Description: Minneapolis : Lerner Publications, [2019] | Series: Gateway biographies | Includes bibliographical references and index. | Audience: Grades 4–6. | Audience: Ages 9–14.
Identifiers: LCCN 2018006098 (print) | LCCN 2018004066 (ebook) | ISBN 9781541538405 (eb pdf) | ISBN 9781541538399 (library binding : alk. paper)
Subjects: LCSH: McCain, John, 1936– —Juvenile literature. | Legislators—United States— Biography—Juvenile literature. | United States. Congress. Senate—Biography—Juvenile literature. | Presidential candidates—United States—Biography—Juvenile literature. | Prisoners of war—Vietnam—Biography—Juvenile literature.
Classification: LCC E840.8.M26 (print) | LCC E840.8.M26 S35 2019 (ebook) | DDC 328.73/092 [B]—dc23

LC record available at https://lccn.loc.gov/2018006098

Manufactured in the United States of America
1 - 45030 - 35857 - 8/27/2018

CONTENTS

John McCain speaks about his experience in Vietnam in this 1973 photo.

Captured by the enemy, US Navy lieutenant commander John McCain had been starved and beaten in a Vietnamese prison camp. He'd had injuries treated without anesthesia. He'd been held in solitary confinement and was terribly ill.

Now he sat listening to a high-ranking official in charge of the prison camps who talked for hours about other camps he'd run and other prisoners he'd released. McCain had been through interrogations before, but suddenly this one took an unexpected turn. The Vietnamese official asked him a question: "Do you want to go home?"

This question was anything but typical. No one with whom McCain was serving had been offered such a thing. McCain knew that he'd been singled out. And of course, he wanted to go home. Yet the simple question didn't have an easy answer.

"I went back to my room, and I thought about it for a long time. . . . I was worried whether I could stay alive or not, because I was in rather bad condition. I had been hit

A young McCain solemnly reflects on his military service, including his time spent as a prisoner of war.

with a severe case of dysentery, which kept on for about a year and a half," he said. "But I knew that the Code of Conduct says, 'You will not accept parole or amnesty,' and that 'you will not accept special favors.' For somebody to go home earlier is a special favor. There's no other way you can cut it."

His mind was made up. He wouldn't accept special treatment and leave his fellow American prisoners behind. He turned down the offer, and for the next several days, the official tried to convince him to take it. He showed McCain a letter from his wife. He told him President Lyndon Johnson had ordered him home. He told him he would die without medical care in the United States. Still, McCain wouldn't change his answer. He knew the meaning of honor and duty. He knew what he had to do to serve his country well. He had to stay in Vietnam.

The years that followed would shape the rest of McCain's life—as a man, a politician, and a leader.

The Making of a Military Man

When John Sidney McCain III was born on August 29, 1936, he seemed destined for a military career. His grandfather and father were both navy admirals, the first father and son to achieve this high rank in the US Navy. John was even born at a navy base, Coco Solo Naval Air Station, in Panama.

John (*center*) poses between his grandfather (*left*) and father (*right*) in a 1940s family photo.

John (*No. 44*) was small but scrappy as a sophomore at Episcopal High School.

Growing up in a military family, John moved around quite a bit with his father, John McCain Jr.; mother, Roberta; and siblings, Sandy and Joe. The family lived in the United States and abroad. They settled in northern Virginia in 1951, and John attended Episcopal High School, a nearby boarding school for boys.

As a "rat"—what Episcopal students called freshmen—John was small but tough. The upperclassmen who threatened younger students couldn't make him obey their unwritten rules. "I arrived [at Episcopal] a pretty rambunctious boy, with a little bit of a chip on my shoulder," he said. "I was always the new kid and was accustomed to proving myself quickly at each new school as someone not to be challenged lightly."

As he got older, John also rebelled against official school rules and traditions. He was supposed to wear a coat and tie to class, but he chose old and dirty items paired with jeans and motorcycle boots. He left campus to party in Washington, DC. He earned the nicknames Punk and McNasty.

Not all of his activities got him in trouble, though. John was a member of the wrestling team and played football. And he found a mentor in one of his teachers at Episcopal. William Bee Ravenel, John's English teacher, talked with him about all kinds of things, including the fact that John felt destined to go into the navy and was nervous about it. Ravenel told John about his own experiences serving in World War II (1939–1945).

"I doubt I will ever meet another person who had the impact on my life that my English teacher at Episcopal

High School did," John said. "I have never forgotten the confidence Mr. Ravenel's praise and trust in me gave me. Nor have I forgotten the man who praised me."

John donned a suit for his senior year photo in 1954.

11

McCain graduated from Episcopal High School in 1954. After that, he spent the next four years at the US Naval Academy in Annapolis, Maryland. He majored in electrical engineering, secured strong friendships, and learned difficult lessons about self-sacrifice and honor. He was following in the footsteps of his grandfather and father, who also had attended the academy. However, McCain wasn't a star student there. In fact, his superiors ordered him to march extra miles for failing to live up to their expectations, and he graduated fifth from the bottom of his class. But he had made it.

After graduation, McCain was stationed in Pensacola, Florida, for a year. He trained in aviation. His education in the cockpit wasn't flawless. He had three plane crashes during his training. He persevered, though, and became a pilot.

As his career was getting started, McCain also had a turning point in his personal life. He met Carol Shepp, a tall, willowy model married to

Carol Shepp, McCain's future wife, in her high school senior photo in 1955

a mutual friend from the US Naval Academy. A few years later, the marriage failed and Carol was divorced. Soon, McCain and Carol were dating, with eyes on a future together. They married in 1965, and McCain adopted her two sons, Doug and Andy. The following year, the couple had a daughter, Sidney.

Captured

McCain couldn't stay at home with his new family for long. He was a military man, and the United States had entered the Vietnam War (1957–1975). He volunteered for combat duty and soon left to fight in the conflict.

In July 1967, friendly fire hit McCain's plane. He escaped unharmed. In October of that year, however, he faced an attack more threatening than any other he'd known. He was flying his twenty-third air mission—a bombing run over Hanoi, the capital of North Vietnam—when a missile flew toward him and hit his plane's right wing, shearing it off. The plane went into a spin, and McCain pulled the ejection handle, hoping to get out before his aircraft crashed to the ground.

The force of the ejection blew McCain's helmet and oxygen mask off and knocked him out. But he regained consciousness in time to land his parachute in a lake. He bobbed in the water, sinking and surfacing to breathe until some North Vietnamese dragged him out. On land he realized he was terribly injured. He'd broken both of his arms and his right leg. An angry mob surrounded him and injured him further before he was loaded onto a stretcher and taken to a prison in Hanoi.

The North Vietnamese refused McCain treatment at first, interrogating him and insisting he give them secret information. He was in pain and barely able to stay conscious. But even when they beat him up, he told them

McCain was firmly committed to the policies and principles of the US Navy.

only his name, rank, serial number, and date of birth. He believed they would give in if he kept refusing to say more. After about four days without treatment, however, he began to worry.

"I remembered that when I was a flying instructor, a fellow had ejected from his plane and broken his thigh. He had gone into shock, the blood had pooled in his leg, and he died, which came as quite a surprise to us—a man dying of a broken leg," McCain said. "Then I realized that a very similar thing was happening to me."

McCain told an officer that if he could go to a hospital, in return he would provide the information they wanted. At first, the officer refused and left. He believed that McCain's injuries were too serious to recover from and that treating him would be a waste of time. Later, though, the officer came back, excited to announce that he knew McCain's father was a high-ranking US Navy admiral. Now the North Vietnamese had a reason to keep their prisoner alive.

"I didn't know at the time that my name had been released in a rather big propaganda splash by the North Vietnamese, and that they were very happy to have captured me. They told a number of my friends when I was captured, 'We have the crown prince,' which was somewhat amusing to me," McCain said.

Moved to a filthy hospital room, McCain endured a great deal of pain as his captors tried unsuccessfully to put a cast on one of his broken bones. The bones were badly misaligned from the injury, though, and they eventually gave him a chest cast instead. They then moved him to a nicer room with a clean bed. They brought in cameras and ordered him to say that they treated him well and that he was sorry for his war crimes. When he refused, they threatened to withhold medical treatment unless he cooperated. But McCain still refused. Finally, they took pictures and filmed him for television.

When it was over, they moved him back to the old dirty room.

An outside view of the prisoner-of-war camp in which McCain was held

The Vietnam War

The Vietnam War was a conflict between Communist North Vietnam and South Vietnam, a United States ally. It began in 1957 and escalated during the early 1960s. By November 1967, nearly five hundred thousand US troops were fighting in the war. More than fifteen thousand had died. In addition, countless Vietnamese people—including civilians as well as soldiers—had been killed or suffered injuries in the war.

In 1968, soon after McCain had been captured, his father was promoted to commander of US forces in the Pacific. Later, McCain's father was ordered to bomb the area where his son was held, and he did it. Though his son might have been killed, he based his decision on honor and duty. He did it to help end the war.

Prisoner of War

After about six weeks in the hospital, McCain was taken to a Hanoi prison camp. He shared a cell with other prisoners of war. But in March 1968, his last cellmate was moved and McCain was left in solitary confinement.

His cell had a dim bulb that stayed lit day and night. His toilet was a bucket. He rarely got to bathe. With nothing to do and no one to talk to, he struggled to avoid endless worrying. He tried to keep his mind busy thinking about history and the meaning of life. Sometimes he made up stories he imagined as books or plays. Even the slightest connections with other prisoners took on huge significance. He and the others sometimes had the chance to tap on the wall to reach one another. They learned that by using codes—such as tapping out the alphabet with one tap for *a*, two taps for *b*, and so on—they could communicate.

It was after his time in solitary confinement, in the summer of 1968, that the North Vietnamese offered McCain the chance to go home. If he accepted the offer, he could leave the horror behind and get the medical treatment he desperately needed. But that would have also meant accepting a special favor, granted only because he was the son of a commanding US officer. It would have meant going against the military and his own ethics. So McCain said no.

From then on, the North Vietnamese guards tortured and beat McCain, trying to get information out of him. When they let him rest, he prayed for strength and courage. The cycle of torture and then periods of better treatment went on for years.

"Finally came the day I'll never forget," McCain said of a fateful moment for all Americans imprisoned in Hanoi. "[It was] the eighteenth of December, 1972. The whole place exploded when the Christmas bombing ordered by President Nixon began. They hit Hanoi right off the bat." The bombing gave the prisoners hope that they might escape. "We knew at that time that unless something very

Lieutenant Commander Jay Coupe Jr. escorts McCain to the Gia Lam Airport.

forceful was done that we were never going to get out of there. . . ," McCain explained. "So we were very happy. We were cheering and hollering."

By 1973 the United States was preparing to pull troops out of Vietnam. On March 15, McCain was taken to Vietnam's Gia Lam Airport. He was finally going home.

"Up to that moment, I wouldn't allow myself more than a feeling of cautious hope," McCain said. "We had been peaked up so many times before that I had decided that I wouldn't get excited until I shook hands with an American in uniform. That happened at Gia Lam, and then I knew it was over. There is no way I can describe how I felt as I walked toward that US Air Force plane."

Living by the Code

Throughout his imprisonment, McCain was determined to live by the US military Code of Conduct. That's why he always refused when the North Vietnamese offered to release him. The Code of Conduct consists of basic principles that all armed forces members are to live by, including

- being willing to give one's life to defend the United States
- refusing to surrender to the enemy
- resisting if captured by the enemy and refusing to accept parole or special favors
- staying loyal to fellow prisoners if one becomes a prisoner of war
- giving only one's name, rank, serial number, and date of birth if questioned as a prisoner of war
- remembering at all times that armed forces members are fighting for freedom, responsible for their own actions, and dedicated to the principles that make the United States free

A Hero's Return

Getting back to regular life in the United States took some adjustment. A lot had changed in the time McCain had spent in Vietnam. His wife, Carol, had been in a serious car accident while he was imprisoned. She'd needed several operations to save her life, and McCain was shocked to find her walking with a limp and much shorter than she had been, due to bone loss she sustained during surgery.

McCain was different too. He was weak and thin. The stress of his imprisonment had turned his hair white. His injuries left him with some physical limitations, including a limp of his own. He also had difficult memories to deal with. He got spooked a few times hearing keys rattle at the door. The sound brought back his imprisonment, when guards would come to question and torture him.

McCain poses for a photo with his family after returning to the United States as a Vietnam veteran.

Civil rights demonstrations such as the March on Washington in 1963 (*above*) paved the way for more rights for African Americans in the decades that followed.

Much had changed in the country as well. McCain was pleased to discover that the civil rights demonstrations he'd seen years earlier had led to improvements in equal opportunity and less racial discrimination against African Americans. But he was disheartened by other changes in the culture. When he enlisted, he believed most Americans supported the Vietnam War. By the time he returned home, that clearly wasn't so.

Vietnam War Protests

While McCain was in Vietnam, protests against the Vietnam War became increasingly common. They began around 1965, but the movement gained momentum over the years. Martin Luther King Jr. spoke out against the war in April 1967, lending strength to the cause.

One of the largest protests took place in October 1967, when about one hundred thousand people gathered at the Lincoln Memorial in Washington, DC. The war became even more unpopular in 1969, when the United States began drafting young men into the military and sending them to fight in Vietnam. Many protests took place on college campuses through the 1960s and early 1970s. Though the United States pulled out of Vietnam in 1973, the war continued within the country until 1975. In the end, the Communists won.

This 1967 protest in Washington, DC, shows the growing unrest about the war in Vietnam.

23

"In prison, I think, you become very idealistic. You get a feeling that in your country, everything is perfection," he explained. "Now that I'm back, it disturbs me to find people so critical of our country and our way of life and our government. I think that many Americans have a tendency to neglect the really fine things and the benefits that we have here and concentrate on the faults."

McCain was grateful for the warm reception he personally received as a returning prisoner of war. The military awarded him the Silver Star, Bronze Star, Purple Heart, and Distinguished Flying Cross. He wrote about his imprisonment for *U.S. News & World Report.* After his article was printed, letters of support poured in for him from across the country.

He worked hard in physical therapy to regain his strength and return to military duty. Restoring his knee was especially painful, but he finally passed a flight physical in 1974. He was soon promoted and commanding a squadron. Still, he could not fully overcome his injuries, and they limited his further advancement. He was not destined to become an admiral like his father and grandfather.

Instead, in 1976, McCain's career took a turn in a new direction. The US Navy assigned him to a position that brought him into politics. He became the navy's liaison to the US Senate. The job gave McCain an opportunity to travel with senators. Telling stories about his experiences and offering opinions on military matters, he began to build strong relationships with powerful people who respected him as a war hero.

McCain's Medals

Each of the four medals McCain received for serving in Vietnam has its own specific meaning. The Silver Star is awarded for "gallantry in action against an armed enemy of the United States or while serving with friendly foreign forces." The Bronze Star is given for "heroic or meritorious achievement or service not involving participation in aerial flight." The Purple Heart goes to "any member of the US Armed Forces killed or wounded in an armed conflict." And the Distinguished Flying Cross signifies "heroism or extraordinary achievement while participating in aerial flight."

From left to right: the Silver Star, Bronze Star, Purple Heart, and Distinguished Flying Cross

Entering Politics

By 1979 it was clear McCain's life was on a new and unplanned path. During his travels, he met Cindy Lou Hensley at a party in Hawaii. She was a twenty-five-year-old teacher. He was forty-three and married. It was love at first sight, though at first they lied to each other about their ages. Each thought the other wouldn't be interested if the truth were revealed.

McCain divorced Carol and married Cindy in 1980. The following year, he retired from the US Navy. The couple moved to Cindy's home state of Arizona, and he took a position at his father-in-law's Anheuser-Busch beer distribution company.

McCain had other plans for his future, however. He was going to run for political office. In 1982 he campaigned for a seat in the US House of Representatives. He wanted to represent Arizona. The odds were against him. Having moved around with the military all his life, he was not a longtime resident of Arizona or any other state. But he was confident and charismatic. He worked hard to win the Republican primary and then the general election.

Serving two terms in the US House of Representatives, McCain wasn't afraid to voice his opinions on political issues. He was critical and outspoken. He was a Republican, but he didn't hesitate to question traditional Republican positions when he didn't agree with them. He began to earn a reputation as a maverick.

In 1986 a seat opened up in the US Senate. McCain ran and won the spot. As a US senator, he experienced

McCain in 1986, the year he was elected to the US Senate

Senator McCain speaks in Nicaragua in 1987.

career highs and lows. In 1988 he gave a speech at the Republican National Convention that helped make him a household name across the country. Many Americans were inspired by his words about making the world safer for the next generation and helping those in other nations who were struggling for freedom. Just two years later, though, McCain was investigated for possible corruption. He had close connections with Charles Keating Jr., a banker who had engaged in fraud. While McCain's name was eventually cleared, the investigation left its mark on his reputation. To do better and improve voters' perception of him, he worked hard for campaign finance reform. He even collaborated with a liberal Democrat to pass legislation called the McCain-Feingold Bipartisan Campaign Reform Act.

McCain was a conservative Republican when it came to military spending, labor legislation, abortion, and gun regulation. But he was more liberal than his peers on issues including immigration reform and health care. His work for a tax on tobacco products to fund anti-smoking campaigns and smokers' medical costs was unsuccessful. Still, it didn't go unnoticed. People saw McCain as a Republican who wasn't afraid to take risks. If he didn't believe in something, he wouldn't support it to get votes.

McCain makes a point in his 1988 speech at the Republican National Convention in New Orleans, Louisiana.

Family Man

As McCain's political career took off, his personal life did too. He and Cindy had a daughter, Meghan, in 1984 and a son, John Sidney McCain IV, in 1986. They had another son, James, in 1988 and adopted their daughter Bridget from Bangladesh a few years later. While McCain worked in Washington, his family stayed in Arizona. He and Cindy wanted their children to grow up in the West. McCain came home to see them on weekends and holidays.

McCain reads the newspaper at home with his wife, Cindy; daughters Meghan and Bridget; and sons John and James.

Presidential Runs

In 1999 McCain took aim at the highest political office in the United States. He began a campaign to win the Republican nomination for president. He ran against conservative opponent George W. Bush. If McCain won, he would run in the 2000 presidential election.

McCain was popular for promising to reform the government and be honest with the American people. But as he pulled ahead in the race, Bush's campaign team began calling voters in South Carolina and asking

McCain speaks at a 2000 campaign rally in Hanover, New Hampshire, as Cindy McCain looks on.

McCain greets UCLA college students on the campaign trail in 2000.

whether they would be "more or less likely to vote for John McCain . . . if [they] knew he had fathered an illegitimate black child." The question made people believe that was how McCain's daughter Bridget became part of his family.

McCain lost the South Carolina primary, and his campaign never bounced back. It soon became clear he no longer had a chance of winning the Republican nomination. In response to the loss, McCain remarked, "I will not take the low road to the highest office in this land. I want the presidency in the best way—not the worst way. The American people deserve to be treated with respect by those who seek to lead the nation. And I promise you: you will have my respect until my last day on earth."

Bush won the 2000 presidential election. As a fellow Republican, McCain supported him, and four years later, he campaigned for his reelection. "I salute his determination to make this world a better, safer, freer place," McCain said. "He has not wavered. He has not flinched from the hard choices. He will not yield. And neither will we."

Torture Ban

Though they were both Republicans, McCain and Bush didn't agree on every issue. For example, McCain did not support the president's proposal to ban same-sex marriage. And when McCain proposed that the United States ban the torture of prisoners, he didn't have the president's support. The president maintained that existing laws already banned torture.

McCain knew what it meant to be imprisoned and tortured in a foreign country. And he believed that certain legal interrogation tactics the United States used were abusive. In 2005 he won the president over to his side to enact a formal ban on torture. McCain was proud of his victory. "We've sent a message to the world that the United States is not like the terrorists," he said.

Presidential candidate McCain takes part in a debate on May 15, 2007.

In April 2007, McCain announced his plans to run for president again. He had Bush's endorsement, and this time, he won the Republican nomination. He chose Sarah Palin, governor of Alaska, as his vice presidential running mate. She was the first Republican female ever selected to run for the office.

People were excited about McCain's choice. But as the campaign went on, doubts came up. The country was in a serious financial downturn. Many Americans blamed Bush and felt ready for a party change. And during the campaign, questions came up about whether Palin had the experience to serve as vice president. People began to question McCain's judgment in choosing her.

In fall 2008, McCain was doing well in the polls. Yet he didn't win the presidency

Palin (*right*) became an increasingly controversial vice presidential candidate as McCain's campaign for president progressed.

Barack Obama makes a presidential victory speech on November 4, 2008, with his wife, Michelle, and daughters Sasha and Malia by his side.

in November. Democratic presidential candidate Barack Obama won with about 53 percent of the popular vote. "I don't know what more we could have done to try to win this election," McCain said to supporters afterward. "We fought as hard as we could. And though we fell short, the failure is mine, not yours."

Although McCain didn't win the presidency, he did distinguish himself as a maverick at one point in particular on the campaign trail. At a town hall meeting in Lakeville, Minnesota, one of McCain's supporters questioned Obama's status as a US citizen, stating that she thought he was an Arab. McCain retorted by explaining that Obama was indeed a citizen, and that he was a decent person with whom McCain just happened to disagree politically. McCain is remembered to this day for speaking out in this way.

Still a Maverick

With the possibility of becoming president in 2009 behind him, it was time to rethink the rest of his career. McCain still had a place in the US Senate, and he continued his service there. He had years ahead of him to keep working on behalf of the American people.

As a senator, McCain remained outspoken and didn't hesitate to question traditional Republican positions. In 2012 he helped to organize the Gang of Eight, a group of four Democratic and four Republican senators—including McCain himself—who aimed to work together for immigration reform. They created a bill that they felt strengthened America's borders while offering a path to

McCain speaks to the media on behalf of the Gang of Eight.

citizenship for undocumented immigrants in the United States. The bill passed in the Senate but failed to get approval in the House of Representatives.

McCain continued fighting for the bill. In 2015 he came up against another unconventional political figure who was also outspoken about immigration—but had differing opinions. Donald Trump, then a candidate for US president, made several controversial statements about Mexican immigrants.

"When Mexico sends its people, they're not sending their best," Trump said. "They're sending people that have lots of problems. . . . They're bringing drugs. They're bringing crime."

McCain publicly stated that he disagreed with Trump's comments. In campaign rallies a short time later, Trump questioned McCain's immigration stance as well as his record of service as a senator and in the US Navy. "He's not a war hero," Trump stated. "He was captured. I like people that weren't captured."

McCain didn't express personal offense about Trump's words, but he did say he felt Trump owed other prisoners of war an apology. McCain said he felt Trump's comment denigrated their service. And he continued to speak out against Trump when the presidential candidate made policy statements that he disagreed with. For instance, when Trump made statements in support of Russian president Vladimir Putin, McCain expressed his disapproval, noting that Putin "has slaughtered his own, murdered his own people." And when Trump spoke critically about the parents of fallen US Army officer Humayun Khan after they publicly revealed concerns about Trump's candidacy, McCain noted that Trump's comments didn't reflect the views of the Republican Party.

A New Battle

In July 2017, McCain faced a battle that had nothing to do with politics. He had surgery for a blot clot, and during his treatment, doctors found he had brain cancer. McCain responded to the news by staying optimistic and looking into treatment options.

McCain reports to the US Capitol for a Senate debate on November 30, 2017.

McCain's funeral took place on September 1, 2018, with many high-profile guests in attendance.

"I'm facing a challenge," he said. "But I've faced other challenges. And I'm very confident about getting through this one as well. There's two ways of looking at these things. And one of them is to celebrate. I am able to celebrate a wonderful life and I will be grateful for additional time that I have."

McCain continued to work and to fight for legislation he agreed with, even if most Republicans disagreed with him. In September he found himself under pressure to help repeal the Affordable Care Act. Going against his party, McCain voted no. He said he believed a better bill could be developed if Republicans and Democrats worked together.

By early 2018, McCain was spending time in Arizona with his family, recovering from cancer treatments. He continued to work, collaborating with Democratic senator Christopher Coons to introduce a bill that would grant permanent legal status to certain undocumented immigrants. In his eighth decade, McCain remained a fighter, keeping up his reputation as a maverick to the end. That year, he succumbed to cancer and passed away, but he left a legacy as a war hero, an unconventional politician, and an inspirational leader to many.

IMPORTANT DATES

1936   John Sidney McCain III is born on August 29 at Coco Solo Naval Air Station in Panama.

1958   He graduates from the US Naval Academy in Annapolis, Maryland.

1965   He marries Carol Shepp.

1967   His plane is shot down in Vietnam, and he is taken prisoner.

1973   He is released and sent home on March 15.

1980   He marries Cindy Lou Hensley.

1981   He retires from the US Navy.

1982   He is elected to the US House of Representatives.

1986   He is elected to the US Senate.

2000   He loses the Republican nomination for president of the United States.

2008   He loses the presidential election to Democratic opponent Barack Obama.

2012   He works to organize the Gang of Eight.

2017   He is diagnosed with brain cancer. He votes against repealing the Affordable Care Act.

2018   He and Senator Christopher Coons introduce a bill that would grant permanent legal status to certain undocumented immigrants. He passes away from cancer but leaves an enduring legacy as a maverick and a leader.

SOURCE NOTES

7 John S. McCain, "John McCain, Prisoner of War: A First-Person Account," *U.S. News & World Report*, January 28, 2008, https:// www.usnews.com/news/articles/2008/01/28/john-mccain -prisoner-of-war-a-first-person-account.

7–8 McCain, "Prisoner of War."

10 Ed O'Keefe, "McCain the 'Punk' Goes Back to School," *ABC News*, April 1, 2008, http://abcnews.go.com/Politics/Vote2008 /story?id=4565619&page=1.

11 O'Keefe, "McCain Goes Back to School."

15 McCain, "Prisoner of War."

15 McCain.

18–19 McCain.

19 McCain.

24 John McCain, "John McCain: One Prisoner of War's Fresh Appraisal of U.S. in 1973," interview, *U.S. News & World Report*, July 30, 2008, https://www.usnews.com/news/articles/2008/07/30 /john-mccain-one-prisoner-of-wars-fresh-appraisal-of-us-in-1973.

25 "Military Medals and Ribbons Chart in Order of Precedence," Medals of America, accessed May 2, 2018, https://www .medalsofamerica.com/content--name-Army-Medals-and -Ribbons-Chart.

32 Ann Banks, "Dirty Tricks, South Carolina, and John McCain," *Nation*, January 14, 2008, https://www.thenation.com/article /dirty-tricks-south-carolina-and-john-mccain/.

32–33 David Grann, "The Fall: John McCain's Choices," *New Yorker*, November 17, 2008, https://www.newyorker.com/magazine/2008 /11/17/the-fall-david-grann.

33 Sean Loughlin, "McCain Praises Bush as 'Tested,'" *CNN*, August 30, 2004, http://www.cnn.com/2004/ALLPOLITICS/08/30/gop.mccain/.

33 Maura Reynolds and Greg Miller, "McCain Wins Agreement from Bush on Torture Ban," *Los Angeles Times*, December 16, 2005, http://articles.latimes.com/2005/dec/16/nation/na-torture16.

36 Jeff Mason, "Why John McCain Lost the White House," Reuters, November 5, 2008, https://www.reuters.com/article/us-usa -election-mccain/why-john-mccain-lost-the-white-house -idUSTRE4A47Z020081105.

38 Darran Simon, "President Trump's Other Insensitive Comments on Race and Ethnicity," *CNN*, January 13, 2018, https://www .cnn.com/2018/01/11/politics/president-trump-racial-comments -tweets/index.html.

38 Luis Gomez, "Trump vs. McCain: A Brief, Comprehensive History of Discord," *San Diego Union-Tribune*, February 9, 2017, http:// www.sandiegouniontribune.com/opinion/the-conversation/sd -trump-vs-mccain-short-turbulent-history-of-discord-20170209 -htmlstory.html.

38 Gomez, "Trump vs. McCain."

41 Chris Cillizza, "The Inspiring Joy of John McCain," *CNN*, September 11, 2017, https://www.cnn.com/2017/09/11/politics /john-mccain-sotu-jake-tapper/index.html.

SELECTED BIBLIOGRAPHY

Austin, Shelbi, and Jennifer O'Shea. "10 Things You Didn't Know about John McCain." *U.S. News & World Report*, October 17, 2017. https://www.usnews.com/news/articles/2007/02/08/10-things-you-didnt-know-about-john-mccain.

Banks, Ann. "Dirty Tricks, South Carolina and John McCain." *Nation*, January 14, 2008. https://www.thenation.com/article/dirty-tricks-south-carolina-and-john-mccain/.

Mason, Jeff. "Why John McCain Lost the White House." Reuters, November 5, 2008. https://www.reuters.com/article/us-usa-election-mccain/why-john-mccain-lost-the-white-house-idUSTRE4A47Z020081105.

Meixler, Eli. "'It's Time to Wake Up.' Read John McCain's Speech to Naval Academy Graduates." *Time*, October 31, 2017. http://time.com/5003525/john-mccain-naval-academy-speech/.

Ringle, Ken. "John McCain, True to His School." *Washington Post*, December 6, 1999. http://www.washingtonpost.com/wp-srv/WPcap/1999-12/06/024r-120699-idx.html.

Vartabedian, Ralph, and Richard A. Serrano. "McCain's Mishaps in the Cockpit." *Los Angeles Times*, October 6, 2008. http://articles.latimes.com/2008/oct/06/nation/na-aviator6.

FURTHER READING

BOOKS

Murray, Stuart. *Vietnam War*. New York: DK, 2017. Learn the history behind the Vietnam War, of which McCain was a decorated veteran.

Perritano, John. *John McCain: An American Hero*. New York: Sterling, 2018. Read more about John McCain's service in the US Senate.

Sherman, Jill. *Donald Trump: Outspoken Personality and President*. Minneapolis: Lerner Publications, 2017. This book examines the life of Donald Trump, with whom McCain clashed politically.

WEBSITES

John McCain, US Senator
https://www.mccain.senate.gov/public/
Learn more about John McCain's political contributions to the United States and the state he served as an Arizona senator.

USA.gov
https://www.usa.gov/branches-of-government
Visit this site to learn how the US government works.

US Navy
http://www.navy.mil/
Do you want to one day join the navy as John McCain did? You can find out more about military careers here.

INDEX